GODDESSES OF INDIA

Parvati the Goddess of Devotion

SHUBHA VILAS

Om KIDZ
An imprint of Om Books International

Queen Menaka really wanted a daughter who would grow up to be the consort of Lord Shiva. She was the wife of Himavat, the king of the Himalayas, (also known as Parvatraj). Menaka went into deep meditation. Finally, her prayers were answered and she gave birth to the beautiful Uma.

Being the daughter of Parvatraj, Uma was also called Parvati, or Himani (from her father's other name, Himavat), or Girija (daughter of the Mountain King), or Shailaja (daughter of the mountains). From her childhood she was devoted to Lord Shiva and finally became his consort.

One day, Parvati was in a dilemma when she found herself alone. Shiva was away from their home in Mount Kailash and no one was around. How would she take a bath, unguarded?

Spontaneously, she created a little boy and infused life into him. How adorable he was! His round eyes matched his round, pendulous stomach. And his loving heart matched Parvati's overflowing love.

'Mother!' he hugged her, sending Parvati in a warm tizzy. After a prolonged exchange of affectionate words and glances, Parvati gave him her instruction.

'My dear son, I need to go and bathe. Will you please guard the gates of Kailash and make sure that no one enters?'

'Yes, mother,' her obedient son nodded enthusiastically, 'I will not allow anyone to enter our home.' As Parvati beamed at her darling, he continued, 'No one, no one, no one can enter when I'm on guard.'

He hopped and jumped and skipped all the way to the ornate gate of Kailash, happy to serve his mother to the best of his ability. Parvati continued to look at him till he was out of sight. When Shiva returned, the little boy was still on guard.

On the gates of Kailash, outside his home, Shiva was accosted by a strange boy. He had never seen him before. Worse, he was actually preventing him from entering his own abode.

'My mother has said no one should be allowed to enter.' He kept repeating the same words over and over again in spite of Shiva requesting him that he was the master of this abode.

When the boy refused to budge, Shiva showed his angry form. He cut off the boy's head. When Parvati stepped out, she was overjoyed to see Shiva back. Shiva too was eager to share his day with her.

Parvati asked, "Did you see the boy at the gate? He is our son. I created him from turmeric paste while you were gone, to help me guard our house. I call him Vinayak.' And Parvati saw the colour draining off Shiva's face.

'What happened? Why are you so pale?'

Shiva could not hide the truth. 'I cut off his head. He was not allowing me to enter.'

Parvati nearly fainted. She loved Vinayak deeply. Within a few minutes, he had completely won her heart. Shiva quickly tried to save the situation and said, 'Wait a minute. I will revive him immediately.'

He ran out and returned with an elephant's head in his hands. Placing the elephant head on the boy, he hastily brought him back to life. Vinayak stood up, and ran to his mother. Parvati was happy to see her lovable son back, despite his elephant head.

Shiva then blessed his son that he would be the most loved god in the world.

Goddess Parvati, the divine consort of Lord Shiva, and mother to Ganesha, is all auspicious. She mediates between the worshipper and the divine. She symbolises fertility and is the goddess of love, marriage and children. Although she shows her power and strength in times of crisis, and rides a ferocious tiger, her heart is all soft and gentle.